A
S E R M O N,

Preached in the PARISH CHURCH

Of *MANCETER,*

In the County of Warwick,

BEFORE THE

Loyal *Atherstone Volunteers,*

Of CAVALRY and INFANTRY,

On WEDNESDAY the 4th. Day of JUNE 1800,

Being the Day of the *Confecration* and *Prefentation*

Of their C O L O U R S,

By the Rev. *JAMES CHARTRES M. A.*
Late Fellow of King's Coll. Cambridge,
Mafter of the Free Grammar School at Atherstone,
Curate of Manceter,
And Vicar of Weft-Haddon in Northamptonfhire.

My Soul *confides*
In that All-healing and All-forming *Power*
Who, on the radiant Day when Time was born,
Caft his broad Eye upon the World of Ocean,
And calm'd it with a glance : then, plunging deep
His Mighty Arm, pluck'd from its dark domain
This Throne of FREEDOM ; lifted it to light,
Girt it with filver Cliffs, and call'd it BRITAIN :
He did and will preferve it.   'Mafon's Caraft.

ATHERSTONE,
(Printed for the Author,)
By James Harris,
And Sold by R. Leigh, Atherstone ; R. Rowell, Rugby ; T. Burnham and
W. Birdfall, Northampton ; H. Sharpe, Warwick ;
H. Gardner, Strand, and Meffrs. Rivington's, St. Paul's Church-Yard, London.
M.D.CCC.

TO THE
HONOURABLE Mrs. DUGDALE,
AND
Mrs. BRACEBRIDGE.

REQUESTED by the refpective Captains, Officers and Corps of the *Atherstone* Cavalry and Infantry, to publifh the following Difcourfe, addreffed to them on the Confecration and Prefentation of their COLOURS, I prefume, *Ladies*, to infcribe it to You, as lending your PATRONAGE, and animating their Loyalty on that Day's Solemnity.

Permit me, to lament with you the neceffity of the Times, which, to borrow the language of our immortal Shakefpear, call for

> "*The Royal Banner, and all quality,*
> *Pride, Pomp, and circumftance of War ;*"

An evil, to be deprecated by all Chriftians, and, more efpecially, by thofe of your Sex, & of our facred Profeffion. Poffeffing every milder Virtue, that adorns the Female Character, and gives Luftre to an elevated ftation, your Natures cannot contemplate, without Surprize and Horror, the Scenes of Blood, which, at the expence of fuffering Humanity, have too long polluted the World. How often then, amid the Comforts of domeftic Life,—while the One is

enjoying

enjoying the sequestered Shades of MEREVALE's Majestic Oaks, and the Other all that Taste can display, in a Modern VILLA at ATHERSTONE,—must both your gentle Bosoms heave a Sigh for PEACE! That soon, very soon, This welcome Blessing may crown your wishes, enhance your own, and the Public happiness; and, progressively diffusing itself thro' the World, in the purest spirit of Christianity, consummate that auspicious Period, foretold by the Prophet,* when, "*Swords being beaten into Plough-shares, and Spears into Pruning Hooks, Nation shall not lift up Sword against Nation, neither shall they learn War any more,*" is the devout Prayer,

LADIES,

Of your most obedient,

And devoted humble Servant,

JAMES CHARTRES.

Atherstone,
July 15th. 1800.

* Isaiah, 2.—4.

To the READER.

CUSTOM and due *Respect* require from an Author, conscious of his demerit, some Apology, however concise, for his intruding himself upon the Public. Suffice it then to say, that the following *Discourse*, containing some *Passages* from other *Writers* upon the same *subject*, was not, originally, intended for the *Press*. After this necessary *Acknowledgment*, the dread of *Criticism*, upon its *Introduction* into the World, is overbalanced by a sense of *Duty*, in complying with the *Requests* of my *Parishoners* and *Friends*. An ardent *Zeal* for *Loyalty* has led them to approve both the *Sentiments* and *Subject* of this *Discourse*; and tho' addressed to *Them* upon a particular *Occasion*, yet, with a partiality flattering to its *Author*, *They* have deemed it not unworthy a more extended circulation.

I am happy in an *Opportunity* of expressing my *Obligations* to my *Friends*; and shall conclude with a *Wish*, that this short *Composition*, being less imperfect, had been rendered more acceptable to those respectable *Persons*, who, by their condescending and liberal *Subscriptions*, have a claim to my particular and most grateful *Remembrance*.

J. C.

Atherstone,
JULY 15th. 1800.

A

S E R M O N.

NEHEMIAH, IV. 14.

Be not afraid of them: remember the Lord which is great and ter-
rible, and fight for your brethren, your sons and your daughters, your
wives and your houses.

IT is very properly obferved that the new Teftament is no
political Book, I mean, that civil and fecular concerns are not
its end or object. The object of the Gofpel of Chrift is penitence
and reconciliation with God here, and everlafting peace with
him in Heaven hereafter. If therefore any Minifter of the Gofpel
unfeafonably obtrudes any political fpeculations of his own upon
his hearers, He difparages his high and holy office; for with or-

dinary

dinary, fecular, occurences, We, as fpiritual teachers, have no concern. But when the general attention is arrefted by new and extraordinary occafions, in which the well-being of the whole nation is involved;—when in fupport of Religion, Government, Subordination and Property againft an ambitious & inveterate foe, who ftakes his very exiftence againft that of Britain, a great mafs of our people, whofe daily occupation is any thing but that of arms, have willingly offered themfelves, and fubmit to the laborious duties of military difcipline, the principles of peace muft in all ranks and profeffions yield to the more cogent principles of felf-defence: the Church of England holds that "Chriftian men may bear arms at the command of the Magiftrate"* We then, tho' reftricted ourfelves from military fervice, confider it no violation of our facred office to adapt our difcourfe to fuch occafions as thofe of our prefent meeting; and fcruple not to applaud, and as much as lies in our power, to promote the general zeal and patriotifm of our Countrymen in arms.

To two Corps of this defcription I am now called upon more particularly to addrefs myfelf; and with fentiments congenial to your own, I feel it my firft and bounden duty to pray for the blef-fing of the LORD of HOSTS, in behalf of yourfelves, my Brethren, and our dear Country, that HE would vouchfafe to profper your

* undertaking

* Vide 37th: Art. of Relig.

undertaking, and the caufe you have voluntarily engaged to fupport;—the defence of your native land againft infurrection and invafion;—trufting, though Chriftianity has little to do with arms, yet arms affumed to preferve Religion, and every thing dear to us, as Men and Chriftians, may not be deemed unworthy of the protection of ALMIGHTY GOD, and moft certainly are entitled to the gratitude of your Country.

To animate the heart of every Britifh Soldier, there is much contained in the words of the text; much my Brethren, which may infpire that refolution, which piety and Religion alone can excite, and which is abfolutely neceffary to our prefervation at a crifis, never before experienced by our Country, by our laws, and liberties. *"Be not affraid of them : remember the Lord which is great and terrible, and fight for your Brethren, your fons and your daughters, your wives and your Houfes."*

From this paffage of Scripture, three fuggeftions arife:

Firft, that of courage and alacrity, in refiftance to our ferocious and inveterate foes:

Secondly, the ground of confidence, a Truft in GOD, *"remem-*
B 2 *ber*

ber the Lord which is great and terrible;" and the refult of the whole is a confideration of the value of the object for which we contend,—*"fight for your brethren, your fons and your daughters, your wives and your houfes"*—thefe fuggeftions being as fuitable to ourfelves, as they were to the Inhabitants of Jerufalem to whom they were at firft addreffed, I fhall proceed to offer fome brief confiderations upon each of them.

"Be not affraid of them." It is undoubtedly true that we have an enemy to contend with, of great fiercenefs, cunning, and implacable animofity againft us, armed with powers, and aided by circumftances unparalleled in the page of hiftory. We know that as far as plunder can enrich a Nation, the plunder of the moft fertile part of Europe has been theirs. *"Before them the land was as the Garden of Eden, and behind them a defolate Wildernefs."** But this fhould not appal us. Plunder and rapine may enrich individuals; but feldom fupply the finews of war. The robbers and affaffins, whom they call Soldiers, may riot in the fpoil of the wretched countries they have over-run, yet little of this reaches the Public coffers; the power and principle then of this deftruction can be but of fhort duration. With refpect to individuals, we have already feen many of thefe plunderers eftablifh a precedent againft themfelves; by the fame rule they com-
menced

* Joel, 2. — 3.

menced plunderers, they have been plundered in their turn : and with regard to Society, the nature of juſtice is eternal, the mad ſpeculations and projeĉts of unprincipled and wicked Men, however ſuccefsful their conſpiracies may be for a time, can never be conſidered as capable of obliterating that ſenſe of right and wrong, which has been implanted in the human mind. If Men retain their nature, faculties and principles, this convulſed and diſtraĉted ſtate of things, can no where conſtitute a permanent government. Society muſt be eſtabliſhed on Religious Principles; and Truth, Equity, Order and Juſtice ſtill be the ſupport of every civil and valid Conſtitution.

The conſideration of *our* happier ſtate, my Countrymen, will reverſe the ſcene. With *us* remains, by the bleſſing of GOD, an Army, that knows both how to conquer the ferocious, ſpare the fallen, and commiſerate and relieve the ſuppliant foe. With *us*, a puiſſant and viĉtorious Navy commands the Ocean, to extend and proteĉt our own Commerce, and annihilate that of our enemies. Add to theſe an increaſing Population, and our Trades and Manufaĉtures flouriſhing, all genuine & natural ſources of Riches, Strength and Security. With *us*, our Nobles, Tradeſmen & Peaſants are armed and united, in courage, zeal, diſcipline and martial array, to proteĉt our property from violence and plunder,

C   and

and to repel the foe, in cafe of any defperate attack on our native Country, the ancient and renowned fanctuary of Freedom and Happinefs; a Country, to which with all its faults, (as a celebrated Author obferves, with the energy of truth and pride of patriotifm,) the whole World is now looking up with envy and admiration, as the feat of true Glory and Profperity; a Country, wherein the exile and wanderer, driven out by the crimes of their own, find a home and refting place; a Country, to obtain the protection of which, it is fufficient to be unfortunate, and no impediment to have been the fubject of its direft foe.

Notwithftanding then "the waves run high," and danger and difficulties environ us, we have lefs reafon to dread the attempts of our Enemies; and that not fo much from our confidence in the arm of flefh, as from our Truft in the moft HIGH; *"Remember the Lord which is great and terrible."* And great thanks are due to HIM, that, though the National Iniquities may be great and grievous, yet, unlike our Foes, *we* have not caft off our Maker. Many of us, I truft, are by the awful events of the times awakened to Recollection and Penitence. By the generality of the Britifh Nation, GOD is acknowledged as their "Rock and Fortrefs." To an Englifh, Heart uncontaminated by the fophiftry of modern doctrines, and retaining alive within it a fpark of the

Principles

Principles which actuated our pious Anceftors, Chriftianity is congenial. *"Without God in the World"* an Englifhman cannot *"find reft for the fole of his feet"*. Like the devout Pfalmift, *"He cries to God in the time of trouble,"* trufting that, *"through God, we fhall do great acts, and that it is He, that fhall tread down our Enemies.*"* Combining therefore every confideration, we perfuade and affure ourfelves, my Brethren, that we have no reafon for defpondency, refpecting the Event of the grand Conteft in which we are engag'd.

You will permit me then to advert to, what, I am fure, you will anticipate, the awful, unutterable Importance of the Object, for which you are now affembled in Arms; that it is *"for your Brethren, your Sons and your Daughters, your Wives and your Houfes."*

In this Nation there are Thofe, few in number, I truft, yet, defperate in defign, who have the Wickednefs and Effrontery to affirm, that we have nothing remaining to us, which is worth contending for; that by the fuccefs of our Enemies, the fituation of thofe in the middle, and lower ranks of Life more efpecially, would be rather improved than made worfe. "Be not deceived; evil Communications may corrupt good manners." Yet, however palatable may be this advice, the futility of it muft, in great meafure, defeat its influence; for devoid of underftanding muft that

C 2

*Pf. 60.—12,

Man

Man be, who can be duped by affertions as falfe, as they are infidious. Could we but fee, for I believe that defcription can fcarcely paint the dreadful fituation of thofe Countries, which the French Armies have over-run,—could we but view the Famine, Murder, Pillage, Infult and Tyranny, under which their devoted victims groan, the weakeft Minds would detect and execrate thefe worft of Enemies, who, by fuch fallacious doctrines, would enfnare them to their own and their Countrys ruin.—Various are the Objects which furround us, and in the wel-fare whereof, we may prefume, that every Individual in the ftate, muft feel himfelf interefted,—our Navy, our Commerce, our Property both private and public.—Are thefe nothing? Yet for thefe we contend, and againft thefe our Enemies vomit forth peculiar vengeance. Are our Manufactures nothing? For thefe we contend. Is the Bread we eat nothing? For this we contend. Are the Wives of our bofom nothing? For thefe we contend;—to preferve them untainted by licentious Ferocity and Infult. Are our Children nothing, whofe fweet innocence we defend, either from immediate Slaughter, or from Slavery, worfe than Death? Should our Enemies fucceed in their attempts and projects—which may God in his Mercy avert!—comparatively happy would be the lot of Thofe, whom the hands of thefe Affaffins might deftroy: moft unhappy the Survivors! Well might the latter exclaim in

the

the words of the Royal Preacher* *"I considered all the oppressions that are done under the Sun: and behold, the tears of such as were oppressed, and they had no comforter ; and on the side of their oppressors there was power, but they had no comforter. Wherefore I praised the dead, which are already dead, more than the living, which are yet alive."* Yet to these Horrors it is not to be dissembled, that there are some of our Countrymen wicked enough to conduct us, if we would follow their counsels;—who under the false yet specious maxims of *Equality, Liberty* and *Sovereignty* of the *People*, have been endeavouring, though in vain, to alienate the affections of his Majesty's Subjects from his Person and Government; and have spared neither labour nor artifice to check that vigour, and break that union, which alone can save us from the galling yoke of foreign or domestic Tyranny.

In our Sister Island indeed, where the intolerant and sanguinary Bigotry of Popish Priests, and the ignorance and blindness of the Peasantry, co-operated with French agents, French principles, and French Arms, the projects of the Enemy were more successful; and though the open Rebellion which they excited, was but of short duration, we have, nevertheless, to lament the destruction of many Thousands of poor deluded Mortals, who could be so infatuated, as to hope for that protection from their French

D   Invaders

* Eccles. 4.—1. 2.

Invaders, which they were falfely taught, that the equitable Laws of their own free Conftitution could not extend to them.

In this wifer and more enlightened part of the Empire, the fuccefs of the foreign and domeftic agents of Treafon and Anarchy has been lefs prevalent. There was a Time,—and the remembrance of it is painful,—when the minds of many, hurried away by the torrent of new Doctrines, betrayed fymptons of revolt againft legal Authority; and the more defperate, and wicked, availing themfelves of that moment of danger, were impatient to work the work of Iniquity, and involve the Kingdom in Anarchy and Ruin. At that period, an ardent and active Spirit of Loyalty animated the Good amongft us to incorporate themfelves, for the Defence of every thing that is dear and valuable to us; and to the Energies of thofe different Affociations we muft, under GOD, afcribe, in a great meafure, the prefent tranquillity and fecurity of our Country. We have reafon alfo to congratulate ourfelves, that thofe new-fangled and ever changing political Syftems, productive of fuch Mifchief and Mifery in a Neighbouring Kingdom, have, in this, been exploded; and, with their Lecturers and Teachers, fallen under merited Contempt; whilft the mifled, learning wifdom from the Calamities of others, are retracing their foot-fteps,—prudently refolving to return to the old paths, in which

which they had fo long, found reft for their Souls. So entirely indeed have the weaknefs, and the atrocity of the modern Revolutionary doctrines been expofed to the World, that if any Man remains ftill inclined to embrace them, we muft either pity his blindnefs, or fhudder at the depravity of his hardened heart. Our exertions, however, againft Revolution and Anarchy are not to be remitted. So long as unprincipled Men remain amongft us, who, to gratify their own paffions, would deftroy the comforts of focial Life, and violate our deareft rights; fo long will be manifeft the neceffity of Affociating in fupport of good Order and Religion. Liberty, without Licentioufnefs, Equality, without Confufion, Reform, exercifed with due temperance, are highly to be valued: but when the meaning of thefe terms is perverted, & the terms themfelves are made the watch-words of Sedition, it behoves us to be upon our guard. The Sophiftical Reafonings which may be deduced therefrom, tho' flattering, abound with danger; and He, who runs, may, from the Ruin of other Countries under fimilar delufion, anticipate the fatal Refult of the Prevalence of thefe doctrines in our own. As long then, as there are amongft us, Thofe, who would infinuate that Refiftance becomes a duty againft, what they choofe to call, oppreffive Laws, and who, flattering in order to miflead the Multitude, talk of the Sovereignty of the People; to counteract the baneful Effects of this fubtle Poifon,

we

we muft ftill, my Countrymen, arrange ourfelves around the Standard of Loyalty ; and the ftrong Arm of legitimate Authority muft ftill be difplayed, to reftrain thefe turbulent Spirits, whofe Ambition feems equal to their Rapacity, and who, regardlefs of the Honor of their Native Land, would fubjugate it to foreign or domeftic Tyranny, with the defperate hope, of either ufurping the reins of Government, or of appropriating to their own ufe a part of the general plunder. But the honeft and worthy part of the Nation acknowledge NO OTHER SOVEREIGN, than his moft gracious Majefty the KING; they know and practife the feveral Duties of their refpective ftations.——They know that the *Governed* cannot be the *Governors*; and that *"no Man can ferve two Mafters"*.*

The late ourageous and Treafonable attempt against the Life of our Monarch——an attempt that has concentrated the feelings and affections of every good fubject,——leads me here to obferve, that it is Royalty, and not the Perfon of the King, againft which the Regicide and Madman often confpire. Was our Monarch, no more than a private Individual, it appears impoffible that he could have a fingle Enemy. Moft exemplary in the relations of domeftic Life, and bleffed with every Virtue, that adorns Humanity, He conciliates the love and efteem of all around Him. There can be

* Matt. 6.—24.

be then no malice againſt His Majeſty Himſelf. Whenever
Treaſon lifts its arm againſt his Sacred Perſon, we may reaſonably-
fuſpect that it is againſt *us*, my Countrymen,-againſt the *State* and
Conſtitution,-the blow is aimed; & whether, in this recent attempt,
the Aſſaſſin was actuated by Treaſon, or by Madneſs, we cannot too
ardently expreſs our National Congratulations, for the Preſerva-
tion of a Life, of the higheſt Importance to the Community; or the
Gratitude we feel toward the Divine Goodneſs, in protecting it
from Evil. Our pious effuſions ſhould be extended farther; when
we reflect, that, tho' for our Sins, we have been viſited with the
ſcourge of a long and expenſive War, *our* being exempted from
many and various Calamities, inflicted upon *other* Nations,
is owing to the ſame Providential Mercy, Our highly-fa-
voured Iſle has not been ſtained by the Carnage of Battles; we live
in the undiſturbed poſſeſſion of our Religion, Laws, Property,
internal Peace, and the comforts of ſocial, and domeſtic Life. Our
People are firm, and loyal; our Soldiery are vigorous, and brave;
our Seamen have atoned, for a temporary deluſion, by rendering
Services to their Country, as beneficial, and ſplendid, as any,
which have been recorded, in the Annals of Fame. It becomes
us therefore, like their pious, humane and intrepid Commander,*
who gave the Glory of Victory to *God alone*, to acknowledge with
Him, that it is to the *protecting Goodneſs of the Almighty*, we, his

E   unworthy

* Lord Nelſon.

unworthy Servants, are indebted, for thefe, and all other Bleffings. Not unto us, therefore, not unto us, but to the *Lord of Hofts*, be a-fcribed the Praife, whofe Arm hath, in all things the Preeminence.

Whatever, my Countrymen, may be the final Event of the awful fcenes, in which the Providence of Go D has placed us; it will be a never failing fpring of fatisfaction to Yourfelves, that the part You have undertaken, and the exertions, You have made, have been worthy the Name, and realized the Character of Chriftians and Britons. Your Zeal, your Patriotifm, and your Activity have been confpicuous; when occafion called to the dif-charge of your duty, you have been found prepared, and your Unanimity holds out a bright Example to every defcription of your fellow-Subjects. Your prefent appearance in this Place, and upon this Occafion, is a Publie Declaration, that you dedicate your Service to Go D, to the Maintenance of His Religion, and the eftablifhed Government of your Country; that you "*fight for your Brethren, your Sons and your Daughters, your Wives and your Houfes.*"

When you call to mind the many powerful Motives, that fhould animate your exertions, for the general Welfare, You will never, I am confident, forget the *fair Hands*, from which, You are, this

Day,

Day to receive your Colours.—The Virtues of domeſtic Life, when They, who poſſeſs them, are living, and preſent too, cannot with propriety be made ſubjects of my commendation; and Thoſe, for whom, in ſecret, the Poor, the Orphan, and the Widow pour forth their bleſſings, which aſcend "as a Memorial" before the moſt H I G H, need no other Praiſe.—The Perſons of theſe Matrons will remind you of the *Sex*, which they repreſent: And be ever pre-ſerved in your remembrance, that a Soldier never draws his Sword in a Nobler cauſe, than, in the defence of that *Sex*, of which, by all the ties of Love, Honor, Virtue, and Conjugal Attachment, He is the natural Friend and Protector.

As the preſent Day commemorates the Birth of our beloved Sovereign, who honoureth G O D, and whom G O D delights to hon-our, I know no better concluſion for the preſent diſcourſe, than to requeſt your united Prayers, for length of Days, Health, and increaſing Proſperity to the Father of his People, the Ornament and Pride of our Land, and the true and faithful Protector of the Laws, of the Conſtitution, and Liberties of Britain. May the ſame Mer-ciful Providence that has, hitherto, been his "Fortreſs and his Shield," continue to guard Him, againſt ſecret Conſpiracy, and open Violence; and diſpoſe our Hearts, as the Heart of one Man, in loyal Attachment to his Perſon, and in dutiful Submiſſion to

E 2   his

his Authority, and the Laws: And when, full of Years, and gratified with every pleasing Testimony of a Nation's Love, He shall, at last, be gathered to his illustrious Ancestors ; may He, then, change a corruptible, for an incorruptible Crown; and may his Royal Posterity, imitating those exalted Virtues, which will confecrate his Memory to future Ages, continue to Reign over a free and united People, in Peace, in Glory, and in Prosperity, until Time shall be no more!

F I N I S.

Printed in the United States
138623LV00004B